About the Author

Ann Grey is an international student who started writing when she went abroad for the first time. Besides travelling and living in other countries like Australia, Ann enjoys her time in Europe when she is home. When she is not writing, she likes to do yoga and going for a run.

Lost in My Own Body

Ann Grey

Lost in My Own Body

Olympia Publishers
London

www.olympiapublishers.com
OLYMPIA PAPERBACK EDITION

Copyright © Ann Grey 2022

The right of Ann Grey to be identified as author of
this work has been asserted in accordance with sections 77 and 78
of the Copyright, Designs and Patents Act 1988.

All Rights Reserved

No reproduction, copy or transmission of this publication
may be made without written permission.
No paragraph of this publication may be reproduced,
copied or transmitted save with the written permission of the
publisher, or in accordance with the provisions
of the Copyright Act 1956 (as amended).

Any person who commits any unauthorised act in relation to
this publication may be liable to criminal
prosecution and civil claims for damage.

A CIP catalogue record for this title is
available from the British Library.

ISBN: 978-1-80074-306-9

This is a work of fiction.
Names, characters, places and incidents originate from the writer's
imagination. Any resemblance to actual persons, living or dead, is
purely coincidental.

First Published in 2022

**Olympia Publishers
Tallis House
2 Tallis Street
London
EC4Y 0AB**
Printed in Great Britain

The Before

we let our past
decide
about our future

clouds

when you are below them
they cage you
you are afraid of them
it's like they take the air away from you
the air you need to breath
they take the light
your hope

and when you are above them
they look so soft
like cotton candy
you want to bite into it
like little grains of sugar
like snow
soft cold snow
you want to lay in it
fall on it
jump in it
like feathers

the purpose of life is to live

I even love you more
than I love myself

you are like a star
you get born out of dust
and when you are alive
you look beautiful from the outside
but you should never come
too close
because you are not what you look like
you are dangerous
if I touch you
you will kill me
not only me
everyone
and then you just die
and other stars get born
out of your old dust

you are the kind of trouble
which I enjoy

that is the end of the story

— because we never had one

I will be the one
who catches you
when you

fall down

even though
you have been the one
who let me fall down

I was happy

— maybe that is what scared me

when I think about it
after all
all what happened
I smile

I dream about
being
someone else
because
I am lost
in my own
body

I am not afraid
of the demons
under my bed
I am afraid
of the person
in my bed
not of the one
next to me
I am afraid of
myself

and the
silence
is my loudest
cry

— the point where you should be afraid

all I see
is my enemies
in everyone's
eyes
because you can't
hide
what's written
in your eyes

I am fighting against myself
and if I win
I still lose

I just wanna get out
out of my body

I feel like this page

— empty

and the
silence
is my loudest
cry

I forgot to write
I forgot to read
it is a wonder
that I haven't forgotten to breathe

illusion will never be reality

Maybe I prefer to dream
than to live

I am not free
I am caged
in myself
because no one is listening
no one
you think you do good things
no
you don't
just listen

I want to be free
I want to travel
to places I have never been before
buying a one-way ticket
and when I want to leave
I just leave
to another place I have never been before
dancing with people I don't know — and will never see again
I just want to be free
and live
I want to live
but I am caged here
I am depressed
because no one is listening
you don't care about this book
you don't care about my needs
because I need to be free
and live

but you don't give me that
— listen, carefully

I feel like a flower
which is withering

The Healing

writing is like a therapy for me
one you never asked for
but one that just occurred

— like you did

I was wrong
I don't need anything
to be happy
I am happy
right now

you are the kind of trouble
which I enjoy

let us rather spend some time with the things and people we love
instead of doing what we hate because someone tells us to do it

and when I'm with you
even years feel like seconds

I started to write this book
because I wanted to say goodbye
and thank you
to the people who are important in my life
and maybe this is why I stopped writing
because I don't want to say goodbye any more

I am writing about you
while I don't even know
who you are

do we really need anything new
if we have everything
we ever wanted?

we will never know
if it was the right
or wrong decision
even though it turned out to be hell
or heaven
or something in between
what would happen if we took the other choice?
there is no real answer to this
no right or wrong decision
just a decision
that may change our life
or it will all stay the same
'cause all we can tell
is the past
and nothing about the future
it is unknown

does coincidence exist
or fate?
are all coincidences fate
or all fates coincidences?

and maybe
maybe she was right
I wanted it too much
I just took what i wanted
but it was too much
it wasn't right
it wasn't right to take
what wasn't mine
to pretend it was mine
and deep inside
I knew it didn't belong to me
it made me lose myself
it didn't make me feel bad
but neither good

— better keep care of what belongs to you

where is this gonna take us?

it is not as bad as it sounds
and not as good as it could be

don't know
what I am doing
why I'm here
why am I going back?
back to what?

to what am I even going
back?
to a life which isn't
worth living

it was better back then

you're like gin and tonic

bittersweet

but still my favourite

the risk about flying high
is falling deep

I am waiting for the perfect moment
but I don't know how to recognise it

if you give up yourself
you give up
everything you ever had

can't move
can't think
can't feel

can't move
can't think
can't feel

can't move
can't think
can't feel

can't move
can't think
can't feel

can't move
can't think
can't feel

can't move
can't think
can't feel

stop.

kiss me
one last time on my lips
on my mouth between my legs
kiss me baby one last time
touch my heart just for
one last time
with your
love

— and let us call the 'one last times' forever

and maybe I am still

lost
in
my
own
body

you are such a lovely creature
your soul warms my heart
and I wish you would be mine

if you can't enjoy the cake
the cherry on top won't help

letting you go
far away
to the other side of the world
out of this town
out of my heart
and hoping
that you will come back
back home

seeing the negative
in the positive
and the positive
in the negative

is it the beginning of the end?
or is it already
the end
of the end?

The After

it took me years to finally be where I am
and I am still not finished

the first

and maybe I just want you
because I know I cannot have you
but maybe I want you
your smile
when you look at me
and the love
you could give me

the second

you have no idea how much I want you

the third

I never needed you
wanted you
I was happy
did not miss anything

but now
since you are not here

I do miss you
and want you to come back

the fourth

you are like a wave
it comes and goes
sometimes it is soft
and sometimes it hits me hard
you are like a gin and tonic
bittersweet
you are like a book
that should not be judged by its cover
because what is inside
is even more stunning
you are like a game
that no one can win
you are like a flower
a scent to remember
you are like a sunrise
full of energy
and colour
you are everything
you are me
and I am you

the fifth

I finally found the person I am writing about

and it feels like this book is only for you

you remind me of myself

if I look in the water
and see a reflection
I see you
instead of me
but I see you unclear
and sometimes
I see nothing
just the never-ending ocean
and I feel fear

the flowers are blooming
only for you
for you my dear
only for you

feeling free
feeling happy
feeling good

in my own body

and all I did for you

I now do for me

I am my daily
inspiration
motivation
aspiration

leaving everything that is not good for me
that does not make me happy

is a great feeling

never thought that there will be an after
that I will ever be here
achieving so much
and I am more than proud of that
and of the people who helped me
thank you.

try to give something back
even just a smile

feeling free
means
being with you

there is no I
there is no you
there is only
us

you don't need to say a single word
your eyes
and that smile
on your lips
tell more
than a single word
could ever do

I am feeling calm
and nervous
at the same time
when I am with you

www.ingramcontent.com/pod-product-compliance
Lightning Source LLC
LaVergne TN
LVHW041540060526
838200LV00037B/1072